20 March – 19 April

amber
BOOKS

ASTROLOGICAL SIGN DATES:
The precise start and end times for each sign vary by a day or two from year to year as the Gregorian calendar shifts relative to the tropical year. The dates provided in this book are correct for the year 2020.

If you are unsure of the Zodiac sign for your specific birth year, visit: www.yourzodiacsign.com.

20 March – 19 April

A guide to understanding yourself, your friendships and finding your true love

This edition first published in 2020 by
Amber Books Ltd
United House
North Road
London N7 9DP
United Kingdom
www.amberbooks.co.uk
Instagram: amberbooksltd
Facebook: amberbooks
Twitter: @amberbooks

ISBN: 978-1-83886-022-6

Project Editor: Sarah Uttridge
Design: Zoë Mellors

Picture Credits:
All illustrations by Fabbri Publications except the following:
Shutterstock: 31 (Elena Naumchenkova), 32 (La Puma), 35 (Slonomysh), 36 (Panda Vector), 40 (Angel Soler Gollonet)

Printed and bound in China

TRADITIONAL CHINESE BOOKBINDING

This book has been produced using traditional Chinese bookbinding techniques, using a method that was developed during the Ming Dynasty (1368–1644) and remained in use until the adoption of Western binding techniques in the early 1900s. In traditional Chinese binding, single sheets of paper are printed on one side only, and each sheet is folded in half, with the printed pages on the outside. The book block is then sandwiched between two boards and sewn together through punched holes close to the cut edges of the folded sheets.

Contents

Introduction

Aries

20 March–19 April

Sign: The Ram
Ruling Planet: Mars
Gender: Masculine
Element: Fire
Quality: Cardinal

Compatibility: Taurus and Virgo
Non-compatibility: Leo, Gemini, Libra and Aquarius

Every man, woman and child is born with a distinct and different destiny. There are no exceptions. Everyone has cosmic significance and a part to play in the life of the universe. This is innate and inescapable, and goes beyond the tiny boundaries of nation, creed and colour.

As we live out our lives on planet Earth, we are, however unknowingly, acting in a greater drama and reacting to impulses that come from distant astronomical bodies, stars and planets millions of light years away. Sceptics pour scorn on the idea that far-distant Saturn, for example, can have any effect on our lives, as the ancient art and science of astrology teaches. But the fact is that we are sparks of energy inhabiting bodies made of the same stuff as the stars, responding like tiny radios to the distant messages they send to Earth.

Each infant carries within it a double blueprint for life: its genetic programming and the pattern of character that comes from the astrological 'clock' that was set in motion at the moment of birth. No one knows the full extent of genetic influence, although it seems to be astonishingly far-reaching, but the power of the horoscope has been well known to the wisest men and women for many centuries.

Our Sun signs provide essential inside information about our destinies. They reveal the secrets of who we really are and why we are here, laying out before us our potential, the sort of joys and achievements our characteristics may bring about, and warn us of problems to be overcome through the triumph of free will.

Read this book with an open mind and discover who you really are.

The Elements

Up to the beginning of the Age of Enlightenment – the modern scientific era – in the 18th century, it was commonly believed that everything, including human beings, was made up of the four elements: Earth, Air, Fire and Water. These were thought of as the building blocks of life, and each astrological sign had a predominance of one or another. Each created its common characteristics, although too much of any of the elements can produce an unbalanced personality.

Fire Signs

The Fire signs are Aries, Leo and Sagittarius. Consumed with passion – which all too often, however, takes the form of self-love and burning ambition – these are the natural stars of the zodiac. They are fired up with motivation, and sparks really fly when they get going. It is difficult to keep a Fire sign doing things at a measured pace (steady old Taureans can sometimes do it, though), because their enthusiasms soon spread like wildfire, catching the imaginations of more and more people. Fire signs are the leaders of the world – especially Leo, King of the Jungle, the most regal and imperious of all the signs of the zodiac.

Fire signs, nevertheless, have great warmth and charisma, and light the way for others to follow. Arians can burn with a cold flame or with the raging fires of revolution. Either way, their passion is based on a childlike – even childish – desire to get their own way, without any thought for the future or the feelings of others. But they are willing to go where others fear to tread, and without them human progress would always be a great deal slower and more difficult.

Sagittarians are the great enthusiasts of the zodiac; they are sparky and constantly generating yet more energy. Just like the centaur-archer and the horse-man of their sign, Sagittarians can rush into things, galloping at the gate that is never going to open magically at the last minute, or shooting very wide of the mark. But they will pick themselves up and start again, uncomplainingly, forever encouraging more timid souls, all while keeping their own eyes on new horizons.

Fire Signs
Aries
Leo
Sagittarius

Colours of the Zodiac

Traditionally, each sign of the zodiac has its own colour, which is believed to be 'lucky' or magically empowered for those born under that particular sign. In general, the colours are associated with the ruling planets and are symbolic of their attributes. Many people find that they feel most comfortable when wearing their sign's colours, and often choose them without knowing their astrological significance.

Aries

Ruling Planet: Mars

Colours: Shades of red, usually the most vivid. Red is the colour of energy, revolution, aggression, war and raw sexuality. Wearing red gives energy and promotes a sense of optimism and motivation, although some may find it too abrasive and combative.

The Angelic Hierarchy

According to ancient tradition, each planet is governed by one of the great archangels, who are also rulers of certain aspects of human life. The box below lists the planet that they rule, the areas over which they have influence and their special day of the week.

Samuel

Archangel of Mars.

Governs: Aries.

Rules: Assertiveness, bestows courage and protects against danger from violence or fire.

Day: Tuesday.

The Genders

Traditionally, the twelve signs of the zodiac are divided into Masculine and Feminine, although of course both men and women are born into each.

The characteristics were assigned to the genders aeons ago, well before modern feminism or political correctness, and may now seem old-fashioned to many. However, the signs do seem to be grouped according to the appropriate gender.

The Masculine Signs

The Masculine signs are Aries, Gemini, Leo, Libra, Sagittarius and Aquarius. Masculine traits tend to be accentuated in the Fire signs, which are Aries, Leo and Sagittarius.

Masculine signs are dominant and assertive, often to the point of being pugnacious, and extroverted. They are natural leaders and rulers, showing fiery initiative, and are fiercely protective of others in their care. They are pioneers and visionaries, conquerors of new lands and the first to achieve great things. They tend to tackle things themselves and can be impatient with others who are less assertive.

Negatively, Masculine signs can tend to be egotistical, arrogant and cruel, and dismissive of the needs and feelings of others. They can also be troublemakers and rebels – violent, belligerent and inclined to subversion.

The Ruling Planets

Until the 18th century, astrologers knew only the planets of our solar system that could be seen with the naked eye: Mercury, Venus, Mars, Jupiter and Saturn. (For the purposes of astrology, the Sun and the Moon are also counted as planets even though the Sun is a star and the Moon is the satellite of Earth.) Uranus was discovered in 1781, Neptune in 1846 and Pluto was first seen in 1930. Many astrologers believe that the existence of other heavenly bodies – such as the rumoured Vulcan, which hypothetically exists within the orbit of Mercury – is about to be confirmed. Astrologers will then have to agree which signs these 'new' planets will rule, and what human characteristics their discovery will accentuate.

Mars

Mars was the Roman god of war, from whom we derive our word 'martial', although the preferred cult among soldiers of the Roman Empire was that of the Persian sun-god, Mithras.

The nearest equivalent to Mars in Greek mythology was Ares. He was seen as the destroyer, which perhaps explains his lack of cult worship. Possibly, like the Egyptian Seth, he was seen as too dangerous to invoke. In India, the destroyer was female – the goddess Kali, who tore men apart in her bloodlust.

The Egyptians had no god of war as such, but worshipped Horus, the hawk-headed son of Osiris and Isis, who represented courage and valour; Sekhmet, the ferocious lioness-headed goddess of revenge, and mighty Seth, god of destruction and the implacable enemy of Osiris and Horus.

Known as the 'red planet' because of the colour of its dusty, eroded, lava-strewn surface, Mars was the subject of controversy when pictures taken of its surface in the 1970s seemed to reveal the existence of artificial structures in the Cydonia region. There appeared to be vast, five-sided pyramids, a gigantic 'amphitheatre' – and, most exciting of all – a 'face'.

About Mars

Mars is the fourth planet beyond the Sun. Due to its extremely elliptical orbit, Mars can pass as close to the Sun as 208 million km (129 million miles), and takes 687 days to circle it. Tuesday is sacred to Mars.

Usually described as leonine, this massive 'structure' looked out into space – as if to send some kind of message for us. However, pictures sent back to NASA by the Mars Global Surveyor in the late 1990s revealed that the 'face' was no more than a trick of the light – or was it? Amid claims of conspiracy and cover-up, Mars continues to guard its secrets jealously.

Arians are ruled by war-like Mars, as are Scorpians (although the latter are now also ruled by Pluto). Mars gives Aries the characteristics of fiery zeal, courage that often amounts to foolhardiness and its explosive temper.

The Qualities

In addition to the influence of gender, the elements and the planets, each sign of the zodiac is affected by having an intrinsic quality – Cardinal, Fixed or Mutable.

Cardinal Quality

Those with a strong Cardinal quality to their chart are, traditionally, supremely ambitious and perhaps somewhat ruthless in getting to the top. They are bursting with ideas and are dynamic in pursuing their goals, especially where their careers are concerned. They see themselves as achievers and winners: every day is a challenge that they willingly accept. Their sense of determination inspires others, although they themselves will continue to take the lead and initiate every new project. They can be dismissive of lesser mortals. Cardinality also represents new beginnings.

Aries

Arians are volcanic in their desire to get ahead and achieve great things, and will not stand for any opposition. Energetic, forceful and competitive, they rush headlong towards their goal and are not above behind-the-scenes skulduggery to get their own way.

Signs and Symbols

Most people are familiar with the zodiac 'zoo' – the collection of symbols that represent the twelve signs. These images reflect the characteristics traditionally assigned to each sign and contain a wealth of knowledge about its true nature.

Each sign of the zodiac is represented by a symbol – the twin fish for Pisces, for example. No one is sure exactly when or why these symbols were chosen, although some authorities believe they date from Sumeria or Mesopotamia, 4000 years before Jesus Christ. The priest-astrologers of the ancient world were the first to impose recognizable patterns on the great constellations – Leo the Lion being one example.

Today, seeing such shapes in the stars may seem fanciful, but thousands of years ago imaginations were more poetic, and many myths were told of magical animals, such as the dragon, which had strange powers to influence everyday human life.

Although the ancient Egyptians left few astrological records, they were almost unique in antiquity for worshipping archetypal, animal-headed gods. However, these strange hybrid gods – half-human, half-animal – were worshipped as aspects of one God. Contrary to the general belief that the Egyptians were idolaters, their religion was basically monotheistic. Each statue represented an aspect of the one true God.

Since they were established, the signs have remained unchanged, although there was a movement in the Middle Ages to change the sign of Aquarius into the sign of John the Baptist – presumably because of the connection with water.

The twelve signs of the zodiac do seem particularly apt on the whole, and accurately reflect the archetypal character of Sun sign types. The great Swiss psychoanalyst Carl Gustav Jung (1875–1961) believed that, deep in our psyches, humanity shares a collective unconscious – a set of archetypal images, which, at a profound level, we all understand. The signs of the zodiac form part of this pool of images, conveying eternal truths to our unconscious minds.

Signs and Symbols

Aries The Ram

Protector of his harem, the ram is an alert, autocratic animal who may look noble from a distance, but at closer quarters can deliver a ferocious headbutt. Rams are strong and tough, but hardly lovable. Those pale blue eyes seem cold and bereft of feeling, yet somehow always charged with danger. Rams often seem like coiled springs: all that energy winds them up to exploding point, then they either fornicate furiously with the ewes in their flock or cause trouble elsewhere. And once they begin to

attack, there is no stopping them: after all, they gave their name to that ubiquitous war machine of the ancient and medieval worlds: the battering ram.

In ancient Egypt, the Sun god Amun-Re (or Amun-Ra) was represented with a ram's head. Hundreds of statues of the god in his ram form line processional avenues at the great temple of Karnak.

The ram was seen as a symbol of fertility, and was often shown wearing a beard, standing for kingship and virility. Even queens were expected to wear false beards on ceremonial occasions to indicate their sovereignty.

The Sun in Aries

Sun sign Arians are feisty, straightforward and adventurous. Blessed with abundant energy and drive, they have no time for laziness or prevarication and make excellent motivators, whether in the workplace or at home. Keen-witted, they see straight to the heart of a problem, cutting away all the unnecessary detail and distractions and are much admired for being quick on the uptake. They are idealistic, eager to defend the underdog, and impulsively drawn to many campaigns for the betterment of humanity, even if they eventually prove to be lost causes.

The first sign of the zodiac, Aries represents springtime, the burgeoning of new life and a great upsurge of energy and optimism. There is a childlike belief in miracles, in things coming right – perhaps at the last moment, just before disaster strikes. Often, though, this blind faith is justified. Positively aspected Arians can be very lucky. There is an attractive naivety about them, a marked lack of deviousness or pessimism, and an ability to find energy and resources inside themselves when everyone around them is burned out. If they believe in something, they will harness all that Martian zeal and go for it, without allowing themselves to worry about the consequences.

Negative Arian characteristics arise out of their driven nature. Often, they seem cold and afflicted with tunnel vision. To them, the end usually justifies the means, even if the way to the top involves methods that are questionable, even ruthless. They are childishly egocentric, extremely demanding and

Personality Traits of Arians

Positive:	*Negative:*
Adventurous	Cold
Energetic	Ruthless
Driven	Egocentric
Motivators	Demanding
Optimistic	Blunt
Keen-witted	Sarcastic
Determined	Self-centred
Honest	

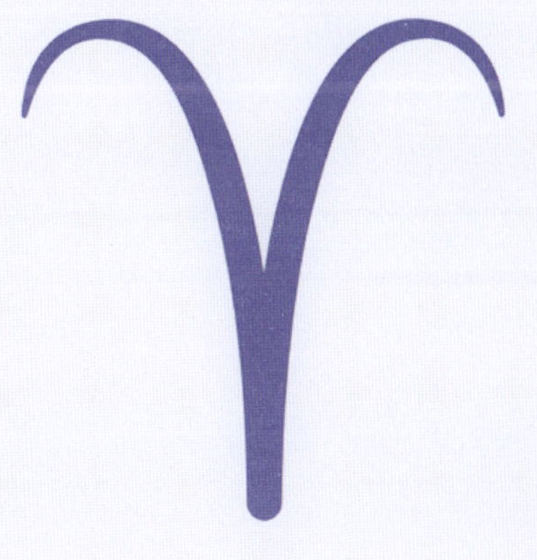

liable to throw violent tantrums if denied their own way. Always leaping before giving even the most cursory look around, Arians often find themselves in deep trouble. Then, they become hurt and bewildered at what they see as the blind force of fate singling them out for undeserved punishment. 'Why me? I was only trying to help!' is a typical Arian response when things fall apart because of their own miscalculation or inappropriate behaviour.

Arians are disarmingly frank, and in their eagerness to let everyone know exactly where they stand they can be very hurtful and over-blunt. They are good with words, but all too often they use them as weapons and can be cuttingly sarcastic and dismissive. Profoundly self-centred, they rarely bother to see themselves as others see them. This is the hardest lesson for them to learn, often at great cost to themselves and those around them. Born under the archetypal Fire sign, Arians can burn up and burn out with equal ease, destroying even their loved ones as they flame their way through life. Many people find badly aspected Arians hard to know and even harder to love, especially when they are well on their way up the ladder of success. It is then that they use anyone and everyone as stepping stones.

Appearance

Typical Sun sign Arians tend to be angular, slim people in early life, although they may fill out later. They have a high colour and brown or reddish hair. Rarely graceful, they seem awkward and ill at ease in their bodies, with particularly sharp elbows and knees.

Health

Traditional Arian areas of weakness are the eyes, head, teeth and upper jaw. Always in a tearing hurry, they often have a fast metabolism, which keeps their weight down, but

the constant speed has its drawbacks, and they are prone to stress. They often suffer badly from tension headaches. Although usually far too motivated either to notice illness or to give in to it, they may be suddenly felled by feverish ailments or accidents, to which they are particularly prone because of their haste and carelessness.

Their Arian impetuousness makes them neither good patients nor natural nurses, and they rarely follow a course of medication or treatment through to the end. This, unfortunately, causes relapses or recurrences of the illness. If given a choice, they may change doctors or type of treatment in mid-stream, not because of indecision but out of impatience. Arians are not good with pain. The slightest twinge worries them out of all proportion to its danger, but they rarely have time to be hypochondriacs. They demand quick fixes or none at all. For this reason, they tend to favour conventional medicine, deeming alternative or complementary therapies too time-consuming and uncertain. Why waste time boiling up Chinese herbs or meditating when you can pop a pill?

Career

Arians are made for adventure, whether it takes the form of dealing with futures on the money markets or exploring hidden corners of the world. Their energy and disregard for their own safety or comfort makes Arians, both male and female, pioneers at heart, willing to put up with enormous difficulties and setbacks for the sake of reaching their goal.

As long as they can be number one, a star in their chosen field, they are generous and inspiring to work with. However, once they are questioned or crossed, their bad temper can make them difficult – even dangerous – colleagues. Well-aspected Arians are public-spirited, as long as they can make tangible improvements and see results quickly. They are impatient with anything requiring diplomacy or tedious committee work. With Mars as their ruling planet, many Arians are drawn to the armed services, where they often achieve high rank and distinguish themselves under fire. They can also express this side of their nature in paramilitary organizations, the police or the Scout movement.

Arians hold strong political and religious views – at worst to the point of fanaticism. They can be either extremely right-wing or left-wing, or they can slip easily into the role of missionary with regard to their chosen religion. They have the dubious honour of making excellent cult leaders.

Anything involving long-term planning is anathema to Arians, and money-making is usually incidental to their ambitions. Typical Arians, who find materialism and luxury off-putting, are better at making money for others than for themselves. They are ill at ease with boring and repetitive

The best careers for Arians

- Police officer
- Marine
- Scout leader
- Army general
- Missionary
- Politician
- Entrepreneur

jobs, seeking to express themselves as individuals whenever possible. They thrive on challenges, and have an enviable capacity to shut out background noise and concentrate on the job in hand. They can be enterprising and excellent motivators of a workforce, but once they are expected to be second-in-command or knuckle down to unappealing tasks, their performance drops sharply.

They find it hard to back down or apologize, although they are usually direct in most of their dealings. However, if they are forced to say sorry, don't expect sincerity from them.

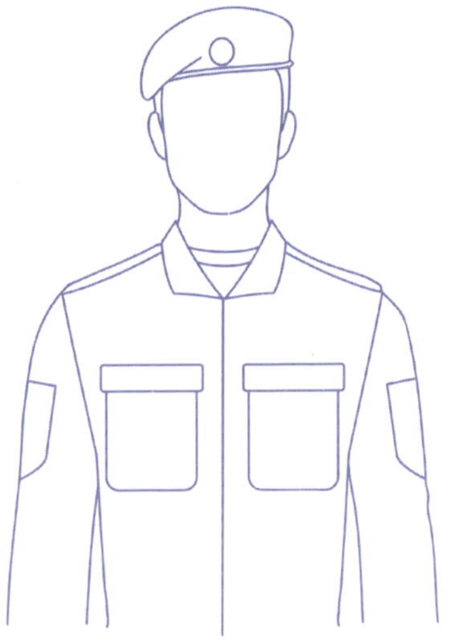

Relationships

Passionate and incurably romantic, both male and female Arians tend to need joyous sex and close relationships throughout their lives. This is a sign of extremes: the pendulum can swing the other way. Some Arians find sex a complete waste of time, although they tend to be in the minority. Most typical Arians find the bedroom either an adventure playground or a battlefield, and they love sexual experimentation, although their basic egocentricity can make them too demanding and selfish as lovers. Incompatibility is often more about a partner's occasional need to sleep rather than a different attitude to sex itself.

Rows will be frequent, although male Arians are quick to make up with chocolates, flowers and romantic gestures, such as a meal out or a weekend break. Always demanding, all Arians will expect, rather than give, support, although they can be motivated to save a relationship if their hearts and sexuality are really engaged. Under their pomposity and bluster, they can often be very vulnerable, and the wise partner soon realizes that they need to be encouraged and praised constantly, perhaps even 'babied' through any crisis.

Hot-headed and devil-may-care, Arians often put themselves and others in all sorts of danger. Never go exploring caves with a lone Arian. All the same, they can be charming, if irresponsible, parents. Some may even find themselves being treated like teenagers by their own children and may be the cause of despair for the more cautious and sober members of their family throughout their lives. Although they will love their spouses, parents and family devotedly, everything begins and ends with their own perspective. Arians rarely ask: 'How do you feel?' The way they approach problems in the family inevitably begins with: 'I think...' or 'I feel...' When their sarcasm or thoughtlessness reduces their loved ones to silent fury or hurt bewilderment, Arians find themselves rudderless, without the resources or people skills to put things right. Fortunately, they rarely sulk, seeking above all to get things out in the open and to let others know exactly where they stand, even if this means adding further to an already hurtful situation.

When romance dies or a loved one disappoints them in some way, Arians can appear to be cruelly dismissive, often reacting by completely cutting the 'culprit' out of their life, as if shutting a door on the relationship and throwing away the key. Always looking forward to the next project or lover, they rarely indulge in nostalgia or sentiment, and they can seem to discard lovers, friends and family without a backwards glance. Any slights cast on them and their integrity will meet with raging fury followed by cold disdain. Arians are unlikely to give second chances or sit down and think about the motives or problems of other people.

Ideal Partner

Arians need support, encouragement and bringing down to earth – with a bump, if necessary – so their ideal life partner belongs to one of the Earth signs, Taurus or Virgo. Their ruling planet, Venus, is the perfect counter

to Martian extremism, softening a tendency to see life as a series of all-or-nothing challenges. Taureans are traditionally no-nonsense, four-square individuals who are conservative and restrained. Fortunately, they often have a secret admiration for more flamboyant characters, and can fall deeply in love with Arian fire. Virgoans can be considerably more organized than Arians, which is no bad thing. However, their introversion and tendency to keep their emotions under wraps can be either intriguing or, at worst, deeply irritating to the average Arian.

Although there are always notable exceptions to the rule, another Fire sign, Leo, is far too similar in character and disposition to be a life mate for an Arian. They would constantly be fighting to be at the centre of attention. Air signs – Gemini, Libra and Aquarius – all too often succeed in fanning the Arian flames, while Cancer, Scorpio and Pisces are either too 'wet' and wimpy for Aries, or they pour too much cold water on all those magnificent, unrealistic Arian plans.

Compatibility in Relationships

Aries

20 March–19 April

Fire meets fire with fellow Arians, and a clash of egos may cause far too many problems for a happy life.

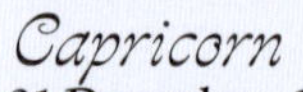

Capricorn

21 December–20 January

Repressed, inhibited Goats may hero-worship Arians, but this combination won't last for long.

Cancer

21 June–21 July

Home-loving Cancerians may offer stability but cause too many scenes. Sometimes it works, though.

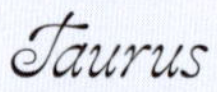

Taurus

20 April–20 May

Calm, dignified and stolid Taureans can give madcap Arians the status and stable home they seek.

Libra

23 September–22 October

Gregarious and fun-loving Librans can suit Arians but the Ram's ambitions can be too self-centred.

Leo

22 July–22 August

Two volatile Fire signs together do not make for a happy life. Some Leos are big enough to compromise.

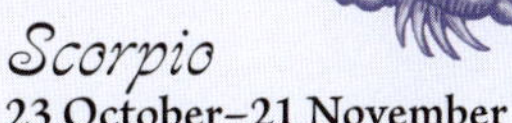

Scorpio
23 October–21 November

Aries will be fascinated by the deep, unfathomable Scorpian, but life will prove too intense for comfort.

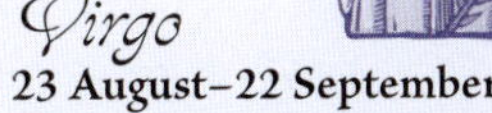

Virgo
23 August–22 September

Orderly, down-to-earth Virgoans can ideally complement Arian fire, as long as they are not too secretive.

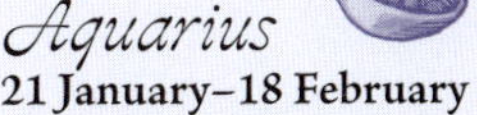

Aquarius
21 January–18 February

Crusading Aquarians can all too often succeed in clashing with pioneering Arians for the centre of attention.

Sagittarius
22 November–20 December

Arians and easy-going Sagittarians do get on, but in the end both will go their separate ways.

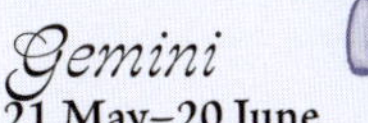

Gemini
21 May–20 June

Geminians tend to be too flighty – and often too wily – for pioneering Arians' long-term plans.

Pisces
19 February–19 March

Dreamy and emotional Pisceans will often find it hard to give Arians the emotional freedom they need.

The Arian Child

Spontaneous and demonstrative, Arians always remain childlike, sometimes even childish. But when they are small children, they can delight and exasperate their parents more than most, being free with their affections but also particularly unruly and headstrong. They are given to foot stamping, tears before bedtime and truly spectacular temper tantrums if not allowed to have their own way. Nevertheless, they also have respect for authority and react very favourably to appeals to their self-esteem such as: 'Who's Mummy's brave soldier, then?' Arians are in many ways admirably independent and energetic. Foolhardy to a fault, however, they are always suffering from cuts and bruises – and more than their fair share of broken bones – so they need to be carefully supervised, especially on holidays.

Criticism and punishment need to be handled sensitively because Arians are inclined to give up if humiliated or rejected. Constructive criticism and constant encouragement, on the other hand, can produce extremely high standards of achievement. Arians always live up to others' expectations. Because of their self-centredness and adventurous spirit, they need clear guidelines for behaviour – the earlier the better. Arians have a paradoxical love of rules and regulations, and once they understand what acceptable behaviour is, they will usually comply with it.

Highly competitive and combative by nature, Arians are not easy siblings to live with, although older children can become brave protectors of their younger siblings. Sharing toys and treats will always be a problem, and the imminent arrival of a baby brother or sister must be discussed with the greatest sensitivity, or the sense of outrage and rejection can scar an Arian for life.

Famous Arians

Leonardo da Vinci

Muddy Waters

St Francis Xavier

Elton John

Peter Ustinov

Marlon Brando

Hans Christian Andersen

Johann Sebastian Bach

Otto von Bismarck

Rene Descartes

Helmut Kohl

Romulus (Founder of Rome)

Leonard Nimoy

Joseph Pulitzer

Severiano Ballesteros

Clarence Darrow

Casanova

Harry Houdini

Wilbur Wright

Modest Mussorgsky

Finding Your Sun Sign (2020 dates)

Aries	20 March–19 April*
Taurus	20 April–20 May
Gemini	21 May–20 June
Cancer	21 June–21 July
Leo	22 July–22 August
Virgo	23 August–22 September
Libra	23 September–22 October
Scorpio	23 October–21 November
Sagittarius	22 November–20 December
Capricorn	21 December–20 January
Aquarius	21 January–18 February
Pisces	19 February–19 March

*The dates provided in this book reflect the year 2020. Dates may vary by a day or two from year to year.